GROSS JOKES

THE HILARITY NEVER ENDS . . .

How do you know a JAP is a nymphomaniac?

When she needs one man a month.

———————————

How can you tell if a woman is ugly?

When her physician is a vet.

———————————

Why do losers walk around with their flies open?

In case they have to count to eleven.

———————————

If whiskey makes you frisky and gin makes you grin, what makes you pregnant?

Two highballs and a squirt.

GROSS JOKES

By JULIUS ALVIN

Disgustingly GROSS JOKES

Volume XIV

By Julius Alvin

ZEBRA BOOKS
KENSINGTON PUBLISHING CORP.

ZEBRA BOOKS are published by

Kensington Publishing Corp.
475 Park Avenue South
New York, NY 10016

First Printing: August, 1993

Printed in the United States of America

TABLE OF CONTENTS

To Paul,
for being the world's most patient editor.

Chapter One:

Gross Racial and Ethnic Jokes

What does "planning for the future" mean in Harlem?

Buying two bags of heroin instead of one.

———————

Why are blacks like vending machines?

They'll always take money, but most of the time they don't work.

If a white couple's first anniversary is their "paper anniversary," what's a black couple's first anniversary?

A miracle.

_____

What's the difference between the average white teenager and the average Puerto Rican teenager?

The white teenager's goal is to make the honor roll; the Puerto Rican teenager's goal is to make bail.

_____

Why is running a sewer system like supervising Polacks?

They're both considered solid-waste management.

_____

How can you tell if a bride is Jewish?

She brings a catcher's mitt to collect the rice.

How can you tell if she's a Polish Jew?

She brings a net to catch the rice.

A guy walked into his apartment and was surprised to see his roommate vigorously rubbing his dick with a one-dollar bill. "What in god's name are you doing?" he asked.

The roommate said, "I've got a date with that Jewish girl I told you about."

"So? I still don't understand."

"She won't touch anything that doesn't smell like money."

Why shouldn't you ever stand in a locked garage with a running automobile or a Polack?

They both emit deadly exhaust.

Why are Italian men so hairy?

Anything can grow on two hundred pounds of fertilizer.

_____

How can you recognize a Polish septic tank?

It has a sign that reads, "Please shower before entering."

_____

What Polish soldiers wear red berets?

They're the elite "Special Feces" unit.

_____

How much money does the average Irishman spend on liquor every month?

A staggering amount.

The Jewish garment company owner died and his widow began making arrangements for the funeral. That night, a friend came over and asked how it was going. The widow said, "Everything is so expensive. So far I've spent $50,000—$5,000 for the casket, $5,000 for the cemetery plot, and $40,000 for a stone."

The friend exclaimed, "$40,000 for a stone—don't you think that's a bit excessive?"

The widow held up a glittering diamond ring in front of her friend's face and said, "Well, why don't you be the judge?"

———————————

How can you tell if the occupant of an apartment is Puerto Rican?

There are cockroaches the size of mice.

———————————

How can you tell if the occupant of an apartment is Polish?

The cockroaches have names.

It was the Polack's first night on the police force. The sergeant handed him a ticket book and said, "Your quota is twenty tickets. I don't want to see you back here until your quota's filled."

Just three hours later, the sergeant was surprised to see the Polack walking through the door. "What in the hell do you think you're doing?" the sergeant cried. "I told you to write twenty parking tickets."

The new patrolman replied, "Sir, I wrote 346 tickets."

The sergeant's jaw dropped. He inspected the Polack's book and, sure enough, the total was right. His tone changed and he said, "Son, good job. Now, do you have any questions?"

"Just one," came the reply. "What exactly is a drive-in movie?"

Three guys were having lunch when one said, "My wife is really talented. She's a musician, and she plays the flute in a symphony orchestra."

The second guy said, "My wife is talented, too. She's a sculptor, and she crafts statues out of clay."

The third guy, a Polack, sat quietly until one of the other guys asked, "Stash, what about your wife?"

He thought for a moment, then said, "I guess you could say my wife is an artist. She draws flies."

The Italian was dragged to Hawaii by his wife and he spent the entire first day grumbling. That night, they went to a luau held on the beautiful, moonlit beach. They sat at a table a few yards from where a man was roasting a pig on a spit. The wife turned to her husband and said, "Now, isn't this wonderful?"

"It's stupid," the Italian said. "See that guy over there? He's too dumb to know that we can't hear his organ and his monkey's on fire."

———————

Why don't Puerto Rican men write many books?

It takes them five to ten years to finish a sentence.

———————

What cards do they accept at Polish restaurants?

Blue Cross and Blue Shield.

———————

Why did the Polish terrorist swallow bullets?

He wanted to take an ammo dump.

Why did the Polack strap a watch to his cock?

So he'd know when it was time to go.

————————

Two black dudes were walking home one day discussing their wives' spending habits. One finally turned to the other and said, "Man, I don't understand how that woman spends so much money. She don't drink, she don't smoke weed, and she's got her own pussy!"

————————

Two blacks were driving down a Southern road when they spotted a stray pig. Unable to resist, they loaded the pig into the car and took off.

They were going so fast that a white cop pulled them over for speeding. While the officer approached, the two men hurriedly covered the pig with a sheet.

"What are you two doing?" the cop asked.

"We was just lookin' for women," one black answered.

At that point the pig stuck its head out from under the sheet and looked at the cop. The officer shook his head sadly, then said to the pig, "What's a nice Southern girl like you doing in a car with two niggers?"

What's a black virgin?

An ugly first grader.

———————

Why do Jewish women make such good tuba players?

Their mouths are so big they can play either end.

———————

Why do Arab women wear veils?

So they can blow their noses without getting their hands dirty.

———————

Why don't black men ever drown?

Their lips are built-in inner tubes.

Why did the birth rate in Poland go up dramatically?

The supermarkets got a fresh shipment of paper bags.

———————

How was streaking invented?

Somebody tried to give a black dude a bath.

———————

An Italian girl saw a girlfriend in a store buying a false beard. "What are you doing with that?" she asked as her friend tried the beard on.

"Can't you tell?" the friend asked. "I've been invited to a costume party, and I'm going as my armpit."

———————

What's the difference between a Polish girl and a bowling ball?

You can only fit three fingers in a bowling ball.

What's another difference between a Polish girl and a bowling ball?

If you had to, you could eat a bowling ball.

_____

What are the three things you can't give a black man?

A black eye, a fat lip, and a job.

_____

How do you circumcise a black man?

With a jigsaw.

_____

Why are American Indian girls such great lays?

Because they're so tight with a buck.

What's a "piece de resistance."

A French virgin.

What does a Mexican man have in the front of his pants?

A Spanish fly.

Why don't Puerto Rican girls shave their legs?

They think textured stockings are still in style.

Why do Indians wear jock straps?

Totem poles.

How can you tell that Italian women are embarrassed by their long black hair?

They wear long black gloves to cover it up.

_____

What do you get when you cross a Jewish girl and a vibrator?

A friggin' know-it-all.

_____

What do you call a black Harvard MBA who runs his own company?

Boy.

_____

Why do black boys have bigger dicks than white boys?

Because white boys get toys to play with.

What's a bathroom menace?

A Jewish man circumcised by a cross-eyed rabbi.

———————————

Why did Miss Puerto Rico win the talent competition at the Miss America contest?

She stripped a Cadillac in 2 minutes, 30 seconds.

———————————

What do you call an impotent black man?

A limp pimp.

———————————

What's the difference between a Greek guy and a suppository?

There's no difference.

How can you tell if a black girl is sexually inexperienced?

She has less than four kids.

What's an Italian 10?

No mustache.

Why is a dresser like a Polish woman?

Neither ever changes their drawers.

What's a redneck?

A guy who will fuck a black girl, but won't go to school with her.

The Irish girl finally got her fiancé to the altar two weeks before Easter. On their wedding night, she put on a very short, sexy nightgown and crawled into bed. But her husband didn't respond.

"What's wrong?" she demanded.

"I . . . I can't make love," he answered. "It's Lent."

"Lent?" she shouted. "To whom and for how long?"

———————————

Why do black men carry monkeys on their backs?

For spare parts.

———————————

Why was the Puerto Rican baby named Juan Carlos Jorge Chino Ricardo Tomas Xavier Pedro Manuel Bernardo?

The mother named him for everyone she slept with the week she got pregnant.

What do Mexican men use as cock rings?

Flea collars.

_____

What's an "election?"

What you find on a Chinese blide-gloom.

_____

Why don't doctors circumcise black men anymore?

They discovered they were throwing away the best part.

_____

What do football players and Polish girls have in common?

They both shower after the fourth period.

The U.S. Government allotted $3 million for a research project to investigate the purpose of the head of a man's penis. The study concluded that the penis had a head to give women pleasure.

The British Government spent $2 million on a similar study. Their results showed that the purpose of the head of the penis was to give a man pleasure.

The Polish Government allotted $120 to study the head of the penis. Their study revealed that the penis had a head to keep a man's hand from slipping off.

Why do black women wear such high-heeled shoes?

To keep their knuckles from dragging on the ground.

How can you tell if black women have big mouths?

When they smile, they get lipstick on their ears.

Why did the black woman return the vibrator her boyfriend gave her?

The first time she used it, she cracked her two front teeth.

––––––––––––

A Polack walked into a bar. The bartender said, "Hey, what are you doing here? Your best friend is up at your apartment right now screwing your wife."

"That bastard!" the Polack screamed, running out of the bar.

To the bartender's surprise, the Polack was back in ten minutes. He marched up to the bar, grabbed the bartender by the lapels, and said, "I ought to punch you. You lied to me."

The bartender said, "What do you mean?"

"You made me run up five flights of stairs for nothing. That wasn't my best friend—I don't even know the guy!"

––––––––––––

Did you hear about the new perfume for black women?

It's called, "Eau de-do-dah-dey."

What's an Italian man's idea of oral sex?

Yelling "fuck you" at women.

_____

A young woman staggered into the police station, screaming "Help, help, I've been raped by an Irishman!"

The sergeant ran forward and helped her into a chair. "How do you know it was an Irishman?" he asked.

"Because," the girl stammered, "I had to help him."

_____

What do you get when you cross a Chinaman with a hooker?

Someone who'll suck your laundry.

_____

What's Jewish foreplay?

A trip to the jewelry store.

What's black foreplay?

"Don't scream or I'll kill you."

What's WASP foreplay?

"Foreplay?"

Why do Mexican women wear long skirts?

To hide the no-pest strips.

What's the definition of worthless?

A seven-foot-tall black with a small cock who can't play basketball.

Why do black men wear wide-brimmed hats?

So pigeons don't shit on their lips.

————————

Did you hear about the black man with diarrhea?

He thought he was melting.

————————

Why do Jewish women only sleep with circumcised men?

They want 20% off of everything.

————————

What's the difference between crucifixion and circumcision?

In crucifixion, they throw out the whole Jew.

A Polish guy walked into a drugstore and asked for deodorant. "Certainly," the clerk replied. "Do you want the ball type?"

"No," the Polack replied. "It's for under my arms."

Why aren't Arab men circumcised?

So they have someplace to put their gum in a sandstorm.

How can you tell a Polish guy from an ape?

An ape peels a banana before he eats it.

A man was sitting on a park bench with a raccoon when a black guy walked up to him and asked, "Hey, what kinda animal be that?"

The man replied, "That's what you've been called all your life."

The black's eyebrows rose in surprise. "So that's a motherfucker!"

———————

What does black-pink-black-pink-black-pink?

A black man jerking off.

———————

How do you know if a JAP is a nymphomaniac?

When she needs a man once a month.

———————

What's the difference between an Italian woman and Bigfoot?

One is six feet tall, is covered with matted hair, and smells terrible; the other has big feet.

What do you call an Iraqi shepherd driving fifty ewes toward an army camp?

A pimp.

_____

What do you say to a Puerto Rican business executive?

"I'll take a nickel bag."

_____

What do you call sex with a black man?

Rape.

_____

What's the African mating call?

"Here I is!"

What's a formal Italian dinner?

One where all the men come to the table with their flies zipped.

_____

Why do Italian men like women with big tits and small pussies?

Because Italian men have big mouths and small dicks.

_____

Why didn't the Polish guy try marijuana a second time?

Because it hurt too much the first time he lit his joint.

_____

Did you hear about the black man who actually put on a new pair of underwear every day?

By the end of the week, he couldn't get his pants on.

What's the toughest thing about hiring a new Puerto Rican janitor?

Showing him how the wastebaskets work.

Did you read about the Puerto Rican social event in the paper?

It started, "Among those wounded by gunshots were . . ."

What do you call a Scottish ladies' man?

A shepherd.

What do rednecks call the first girl they screw?

Sis.

Why do black men have such strong arms?

Color TVs keep getting heavier.

Why did the black dude hold a lighter under his girlfriend's vagina?

He was trying to smoke her crack.

A Polack went to the bordello and said to the madam, "I want to sleep with Irma."

The madam went over to the blonde, talked for a moment, then said, "Irma wants $200."

"But it was only $50 last time."

The madam shrugged. "Take her or leave her."

The Polack paid the money and took Irma upstairs. Afterwards, when he was putting his pants on, he asked the whore, "Well, how was I?"

Irma replied, "You're absolutely the worst lay I ever had in my life, just like I told you the last time. I can't understand why you came back?"

"I wanted a second opinion," replied the Polack.

Why did the Polack wait until he was sixty-four years old to screw his wife?

He'd heard that most married couples have sex just before retiring.

Did you hear that Bill Cosby wrote a special edition of his book *Fatherhood* for black men?

It's called *Fuck and Run.*

Why did the Polish woman douche with Crest?

Crest reduces cavities.

Why shouldn't you eat a Polish woman?

You can get trichinosis from gnawing on a pig.

Why is an Italian woman like a hockey goalie?

They both change their pads after every three periods.

_____

Why did the dentist charge double for the black chick?

She had the biggest cavity he ever drilled.

_____

What's the only reason JAPs marry?

Vibrators don't give you American Express Cards.

_____

Why did the Polack trade an outhouse for his wife?

The hole was smaller and it smelled better.

What's the difference between a JAP and a volcano?

A volcano doesn't fake eruptions.

———————————

How does a JAP eat a banana?

Under duress.

———————————

Why doesn't a JAP breast-feed male children?

They might become leeches like her husband.

———————————

What do you get when you cross a JAP with a hooker?

A woman who goes down on credit cards.

Why do JAPs like wonton soup?

Because wonton spelled backwards is "not now."

_____

What's the difference between a JAP and poverty?

Poverty sucks.

_____

How much does it cost to divorce a JAP?

It doesn't matter. It's worth it.

_____

Why does a JAP have so many wrinkles around her eyes?

From squinting and asking, "Suck what?"

What does a JAP do to keep her hands so soft and her fingernails so long and perfect?

Absolutely nothing.

Two Jewish guys met in a bar when one asked, "Did you hear that poor Saul Weinstein killed himself?"

"No. Why?"

"His wife spent so much money he was facing bankruptcy."

"How did he die?" the second guy asked.

"Broken neck. He piled up all his wife's clothes, then jumped off the top."

Did you hear about the JAP who didn't recover from plastic surgery?

Her husband cut up her credit cards.

How can you tell if a Polack is cultured?

He takes the dishes out of the sink before he pisses in it.

_____

Where's the safest place to hide money from a JAP?

Under the vacuum cleaner.

_____

Why is a JAP like a tampon?

They're both stuck up cunts.

A Texas oil man went to court and demanded a divorce from his adulterous wife.

"On what grounds?" the judge asked.

"Breach of contract."

"Come on, now," the judge admonished. "You don't own your wife as if she were a piece of property."

"Maybe not," the Texan said. "But I damn sure have exclusive drilling rights."

A Texan walked into an expensive restaurant and ordered a glass of vintage wine and a piece of limburger cheese. The waiter's eyebrows rose in astonishment, but he complied with the request.

The man drank one glass of wine, but didn't touch the cheese. He consumed a second, then a third glass, but still left the limburger alone. Finally, the waiter's curiosity got the best of him.

"Pardon me, sir," the waiter said, "but I can't help wondering why you ordered such a stinking cheese with such fine wine?"

"It's sentiment," the Texan replied. "When I drink wine at home, my wife's sitting next to me."

Did you hear about the WASP wives flocking to the store to buy a new product called SEX-LAX?

It's for men who have trouble coming instead of going.

———————————

When her husband died, the funeral director, a family friend, came to the widow and asked, "Jane, is there anything I can do?"

Parting her veil, the widow whispered a request. The funeral director turned bright red and refused. But she continued to badger him until he gave in. "I'll do it tomorrow," he said.

The next day, the funeral director dropped a paper bag off at her house. The widow popped the contents into a pot of boiling water. A few moments later, a neighbor came by, peered into the pot, then said in a shocked tone, "Jane, I can't believe it. Is that a man's penis in there?"

"That's my husband's prick," Jane replied. "All his life I had to eat it his way. Now that's he dead, I'm gonna eat it mine."

When the JAP asked her husband what he wanted for his birthday, the guy replied, "A blow job." The idea of oral sex had always repulsed her, but she listened to his arguments. "Listen," he said. "If you do this for me just one time, I'll respect you forever. Your generosity will be enshrined in my heart. I promise." She was still embarrassed, but finally gave in.

They went into the bedroom. He sat on the edge of the bed while she knelt in front of him and went to work. A couple of minutes later the phone rang. He reached for the phone, said hello, then handed the phone to his wife. "It's for you, cocksucker," he said.

———————

The mortician was laying out the body of a black man with an unbelievably long penis. He called in his receptionist to show her. She took a look, then said, "That's just like my husband's."

The mortician asked, "You mean he's got one that long?"

"No," she replied. "That dead."

What do you call a JAP who finds no fault with her husband?

A widow.

_____

How can you tell if a guy is Scottish?

He sleeps with his mother-in-law to save wear and tear on his wife.

Chapter Two:

Gross Celebrity Jokes

Why was the 1992 Democratic Presidential ticket "R-rated?"

Too much sex and Gore.

The wealthy industrialist suffered a heart attack and was confined to bed for several weeks. One day his doctor came to see him and said, "I've got some good news and some bad news."

The rich patient said, "Give me the good news first."

The doctor said, "I was wrong about your prognosis. You've bounced back amazingly well. As I told your wife a few minutes ago, although you'll have to stay in bed or use a wheelchair, I think you've got some time ahead of you."

"That's terrific," the man exclaimed. "What could possibly be the bad news?"

The doctor said, "Your wife just fired me. Your new doctor's name is Kevorkian."

———————

Why did Snow White eat the poisoned apple?

Anything was better than giving seven blow jobs a night.

———————

Why was *Batman Returns* rated X?

We see the Caped Crusader kissing a pussy.

Why is Catwoman like a real cat?

You're likely to find either one eating Robin.

—————————

What's so unusual about having drinks at the World Trade Center?

You stay sober, but your car gets bombed.

—————————

Why did the Los Angeles police officers leave the ball game early?

They wanted to beat the crowd.

—————————

What did Woody Allen do when he got really depressed?

He went to one of Mia Farrow's daughters and had her blow his brains out.

What goes into 19 twice?

Woody Allen.

_____

What's the basic problem with the Clintons' marriage?

Hillary Rodham wants to be the Rodman.

_____

Why was Bill Clinton so anxious to move his family to Washington?

In Arkansas, Chelsea would be married and pregnant at thirteen.

_____

What do Ross Perot and a Yugo have in common?

They're both small and ugly, and you never know when they're going to quit on you.

Why shouldn't we be surprised when shrinks have sex with their patients?

What other kind of person would use the term "The-rapist."

———————————

Warren Beatty was killed in a car crash. A moment later he appeared in the Hereafter, where the Devil was waiting for him. "We're honored to have a celebrity with us," Satan said. "How'd you like a tour?"

"Sounds good," the movie star replied. They walked along, and Beatty's eyes grew wide as he saw rooms filled with men sitting at tables covered with fine wine bottles while gorgeous women sat in their laps. He finally turned to the Devil and said, "I had no idea Hell would be like this."

The Devil smiled. "Don't get the wrong idea. See those wine bottles? They all have holes in the bottom." He paused, then continued. "See those women? They don't!"

———————————

Why is the U.S. economy like a wet dream?

They're both coming unscrewed.

One Friday night around midnight Bill Clinton wandered over to the executive offices and discovered his young staffers were throwing a wild party. He saw that a white sheet with a hole in it had been strung across one of the offices. A secretary explained, "The guys took turns sticking their dicks through the hole, and we had to guess their identity."

The President said, "Sounds like fun. Wish I'd been here."

"You should have been," the girl replied. "You name came up eight times."

———————

What do Bill Clinton and baseball pitchers have in common?

Fast balls.

———————

What's Woody Allen's favorite song?

"Thank Heaven for Little Girls."

What's his second favorite song?

"Baby Love."

Did you hear about the world's dumbest mosquito?

He bit Madonna on the arm.

What's brown and sits in the woods?

Winnie's Pooh.

Did Adolf Hitler wipe his ass with his left hand or his right hand?

With toilet paper—he wasn't that crazy.

What do you call a bisexual bathroom?

Elton John.

What was Humpty Dumpty's last thought?

"Oh, my goodness, I'm not wearing clean underwear."

Did you hear that Liberace and Rudolph Nureyev died of food poisoning?

They ate a few bad wienies.

Did you hear about Evil Knieval's latest stunt?

He's going to run across Somalia with a sandwich strapped to his back.

What do you get when you cross a cat with Mick Jagger?

A pussy with big lips.

Chapter Three:

Gross Jokes about Homosexuals

How can you tell if a guy is gay?

The only way he'll check his appearance is in a rearview mirror.

_____

How do you know if you're in a group of pedophiles?

You can't separate the men from the boys.

Why should you be suspicious of a guy if he passes a lot of gas?

Farts are homosexual mating calls.

Two lesbians were standing at the bar drinking when another girl waved from across the room. "Who is that chick?" one said to the other. "I'd sure like to get her spread out on my sheets."

"No, you wouldn't," the other lesbian said. "She's hung like a doughnut."

What do you call gay romance novels?

Fairy tales.

Why do so many gay men have mustaches?

To hide the stretch marks.

Why did the lesbian end up in a prison hospital?

She was picked up by the fuzz.

_____

When are lesbians good at softball?

When they swing both ways.

_____

How can you tell a guy's into anal sex?

When he's always trying to enlarge the circle of his friends.

_____

Why don't lesbians travel abroad?

After a couple of days, they miss their native tongue.

Why do lesbians hang out in hardware stores?

They just love Snap-On Tools.

———————————

What's latent homosexuality?

Swishful thinking.

———————————

What's a lesbian cocktail lounge?

A her-she bar.

———————————

Why didn't the fag know who gave him AIDS?

You think he's got eyes in the back of his head?

How can you tell if a guy is bisexual?

When he likes girls as well as the next fellow.

How can you tell if a college guy is gay?

If he spends his junior year a broad.

What's the difference between a bull dyke and a whale?

About five pounds and a flannel shirt.

How can you tell if a woman who walks into a bar is a dyke?

If she offers to lick everyone in the house.

How can you tell if a church has a gay congregation?

Only half the worshipers are kneeling.

———————————

What do you call a lesbian's IUD?

A fruit loop.

———————————

How can you tell a lesbian bar?

Even the pool tables don't have balls.

———————————

Why are lesbians so popular?

Other women eat her up and no man is down on her.

What does a lesbian do when her secretary makes a mistake?

Gives her a tongue lashing.

_____

How can you tell if a woman is a lesbian?

She wants to eat out every night.

_____

What do lesbians bring to work?

Box lunches.

_____

Did you hear about the gay Marine sergeant?

They caught him drilling his privates.

Why are most homosexuals pricks?

You are what you eat.

Did you hear about the new designer pants for homosexuals?

The zipper's in the rear.

What's a shit?

A faggot's wet dream.

How can you tell if a house belongs to a homosexual?

The doormat reads, "Wipe your knees."

How can you tell a homosexual novel?

The hero always gets his man in the end.

What's a gay Western?

A movie in which all the good guys are hung.

Why are gay men the most social people in the world?

They all have friends up the ass.

Why can't gays get auto insurance?

They get rear-ended too often.

How do male prostitutes do?

They make piles.

Chapter Four:

Gross Senior Citizen Jokes

What's the most useless thing in Grandma's house?

Grandpa's thing.

_____

One guy said to another, "The woman I saw you with last night must have been over sixty years old. What's the story?"

"I love women that age," the other man replied. "They don't swell, they don't tell, they don't smell, and they're grateful as hell."

Did you hear about the old woman who had her face lifted eleven times?

If she has it done once more, she'll be a bearded lady.

––––––––––––––––

Why do so many old women go without a bra?

Their tits sag so much it takes the wrinkles out of their faces.

––––––––––––––––

The elderly couple were listening to a religious program when the preacher called out, "God will heal you all. Just stand up, put one hand on the radio, and place the other hand on the part of your body that's sick."

The old woman got to her feet, put one hand on the radio and the other on her arthritic hip. The old man put one hand on the radio and the other on his cock.

"Don't be foolish, Fred," the old woman snapped. "The preacher said God would heal the sick, not raise the dead!"

What's optimism?

A seventy-five-year-old woman who still shaves her legs.

Why did the little old lady with varicose veins win first prize at the costume ball?

She took off all her clothes and went as a road map.

A ninety-year-old woman and a ninety-five-year-old man had just gotten married. When the husband tottered out of the bathroom ready for bed, he found his wife standing on her head, naked, up against the wall.

"What in tarnation are you doing?" he demanded.

"Well," she explained. "I figured if you couldn't get it up, you could just drop it in."

A girl of eighteen ran into her friend, and the friend asked how married life was going with her eighty-year-old husband.

"Oh," said the teenager, "it's the same old thing, weak in, weak out."

A guy walked into the whorehouse to find all the hookers taken—except one decidedly older lady with grey hair. He almost passed, but he was so horny, he decided to go ahead.

They were in the sack going at it for about fifteen minutes when the whore whispered in his ear, "Baby, there may be winter in my hair but there's summer in my heart."

The john grunted. "Lady, there may be summer in your heart, but if you don't get some spring in your ass, we'll be here until fall."

The sixty-nine-year-old millionaire was sitting in the bar of his club talking to a friend. The millionaire confessed he was in love with a twenty-two-year-old dancer. "Tell me honestly," he asked, "do you think I have a better chance of marrying her if I tell her I'm fifty-five?"

His friend replied, "I think you've got a better chance if you tell her you're eighty."

———————

The eighty-four-year-old man went to the doctor for a pre-nuptial checkup. He said, "Doctor, my future bride wants you to find out if I'm sexually fit."

"All right," the physician said. "Show me your sex organ."

The old man held up his index finger and stuck out his tongue.

———————

A tourist stopped at a rural country store for a soda on a hot day. He fell into a conversation with an old man rocking on the porch. After a while he asked, "Pop, can you remember the first girl you ever screwed?"

The old man snorted. "The first? Hell, sonny, I can't even remember the last one."

Did you hear about the ninety-one-year-old man who was acquitted of rape?

The evidence wouldn't stand up in court.

Elihu, age eighty-nine, hobbled with his cane through the door of the whorehouse. The madam looked at him in disbelief, then said, "Pop, why are you here?"

"Want a girl," Elihu said. "I want to get fucked."

"How old are you?" she asked.

He told her.

"Eighty-nine?" the madam repeated. "Pop, you've had it."

"I have?" he replied. He reached for his wallet and asked, "How much do I owe?"

What's the worst thing about being an old man these days?

The sexual revolution has arrived, but you've run out of ammunition.

What happened to the old maid who got tired of using candles?

She called in an electrician.

————————————

A salesman was staying in an old hotel where the bathrooms were down the hall. He awoke before dawn with a full bladder. He didn't have a bathrobe, so he chanced a naked dash to the bathroom. But halfway down the hall, a door opened and three old maids came out of their room.

The salesman froze like a statue. The first old maid looked at him and put a nickel in his mouth. The second old maid put a dime in his mouth. The third old maid put a quarter in his mouth and grabbed his penis. "Look," she told her friends, "it dispenses hand lotion!"

The old maid was given a surprise birthday party by her nieces and nephews. They brought in the blazing birthday cake. The old maid started to cut the cake, but a niece stopped her, saying, "Aunt Elsie, you're supposed to make a wish, blow out the candles, and take them out of the cake."

"I know," she snapped. "But if I get my wish, I won't need the candles."

The seventy-year-old man met a friend on the street who asked him what he'd been doing lately. "I just spent six months in jail on a rape charge," the old man admitted.

"Rape?" questioned the first man. "At your age?"

"I know it's ridiculous," the old man said. "But I was so flattered by the accusation I pled guilty."

The eighty-year-old tycoon married his twenty-one-year-old secretary. They got to the bridal suite about 8:00 P.M., and the secretary waited nervously in bed until the old man tottered out in his nightshirt. He turned to his bride and held up five fingers.

Startled, she asked, "You mean you want to do it five times?"

"No," he said. "I want you to pick a finger."

————————

Why do old women wear black garters?

In memory of those who have passed beyond.

————————

What does it mean when an old man dates a young girl?

He needs to be Pampered.

Did you hear about the old man who had sex almost every night?

Almost Monday night, almost Tuesday night, almost Wednesday night . . .

What's the difference between an old man and a penis?

When you stroke a penis, the wrinkles come out.

The old man told his wife that it was time to go to town to apply for Social Security. His wife said, "You don't have a birth certificate. How are you going to prove how old you are?"

The man told her not to worry. And sure enough, he arrived back home a few hours later with his first check.

"What did you do," his wife asked him.

"I just unbuttoned my shirt and showed them the grey hairs on my chest," the old man said.

His wife grimaced. "Then why didn't you drop your trousers and apply for disability?"

Did you hear about the eighty-year-old man who was arrested for trying to rape a nineteen-year-old girl?

The charge was "assault with a dead weapon."

_____

Why are old men like bumper stickers?

They're both very hard to get off.

_____

Why should you divorce your husband when he turns sixty-five?

Because it's awful to feel old age creeping up on you.

The old man found his life very dull as years went on. He saved some money each week until he had $100. Then he went out and bought himself a very fancy, gleaming pair of alligator shoes. He put the shoes on, rushed home, walked in the door, and said to his wife, "Sophie, do you notice anything different about me?"

She just shrugged.

He went into the bedroom, took off his coat, jacket, and hat and came back out into the living room. "Well, Sophie, what do you see now?"

She glanced over and said in a bored voice, "I told you, I don't see anything different."

Frustrated, he went back into the bedroom and took off every stitch of clothing except his shoes. He returned to his wife and demanded, "Now, you've gotta notice."

Sophie said, "All I see is the same old limp dick."

"That limp dick is pointing towards a brand new $100 pair of alligator shoes."

Sophia grimaced. "Better you should have bought a $100 hat."

_____

Did you hear about the eighty-seven-year-old man with the horrible case of VD?

All his fingers fell off.

Did you hear about the new Senior Citizen edition of Trivial Pursuits?

The hardest question is, "Where did you leave your teeth?"

Chapter Five:

Gross Jokes about Ugly Women

What do ugly girls wear in their lockets?

A picture of a candle.

———————

What do ugly girls do for exercise?

They do push-ups in the cucumber patch.

What do ugly broads use as underarm deodorant?

Raid.

———————————

Why don't they let ugly broads swim in lakes?

Ten minutes after they jump in, the water's covered with dead fish.

———————————

How can you tell if an ugly girl is having her period?

She's only wearing one white sock.

———————————

What do a football and an ugly girl have in common?

Pigskin.

How can you tell if an ugly girl is desperate?

She sends change-of-address cards to peeping Toms.

_____

What's the difference between an ugly girl and garbage?

Garbage gets picked up.

_____

Did you hear about the college that had separate dorms for ugly girls?

They're called pig sties.

_____

What's the only way ugly girls can get appointments with a plastic surgeon?

Blind date.

Why do ugly women end up driving old cars?

Because it's easy to get screwed by a used-car sales-man.

_____

What's the difference between a dog and a fox?

About a six-pack.

_____

What's the definition of frustration?

When your date puts her bra on backwards and it fits.

_____

What do they call the new sex club in New York City that attracts ugly women?

Pluto's Retreat.

A butcher's daughter was fast becoming an old maid. She'd turned thirty, and she refused to date, causing her father no end of worry.

One night, however, the butcher heard his daughter sneak out of her room. He got up and followed her downstairs, hoping she was meeting a man. Instead, he saw her masturbating furiously with a piece of bratwurst from the meat case.

The next day, the butcher was behind the counter when a customer pointed to the bratwurst and asked, "How much is that?"

The butcher grunted, then replied. "That's not for sale. That's my son-in-law."

An ugly girl went to the doctor and admitted that she'd tried to pay men to have sex with her. But all of them fled, complaining that her cunt stank. She couldn't see how that could be true, because when she bent over, she couldn't smell a thing.

The docor examined her, then said, "You need an operation."

"On my pussy?" she asked.

"On your nose," the doctor replied.

What's a lap dog?

An ugly woman who gives head.

_____

Why did the ugly girl have her zip code tatooed on her thighs?

She hoped to get some male in her box.

_____

What's the most important sex aid when you're screwing an ugly girl?

Pepto Bismol.

_____

How do you make paper dolls?

Screw an old bag.

What do fat girls and mopeds have in common?

They're both fun to ride until a friend sees you.

_____

What's an ugly girl?

A do-it-yourself expert.

_____

What does an ugly girl call the pickle she uses to satisfy herself?

Her birth control dill.

_____

How can you tell if a girl is ugly?

When you don't know whether to shake her hand or sniff her ass.

How do you tell if a girl is ugly?

When she looks like she ran out of money halfway through a sex-change operation.

How can you tell if a girl is ugly?

When her personal physician is a vet.

What's the ultimate embarrassment for an ugly woman?

Taking her German Shepherd to the vet and being told he has the clap.

Why do ugly girls get tired of their sex lives?

It's the same thing, wick in and wick out.

Two ugly women were walking into town when a man leaped out of the bushes. He pulled one to the ground and raped her. When it was over, the woman asked her friend. "What are we going to do? How can I explain to the police I was raped twice in one night?"

"Twice?" her puzzled friend asked.

"Well, we are coming back this way, aren't we?"

———————

The ugly woman was mugged on a dark street. She explained that she had no money, but the mugger insisted that it must be in her bra, and he started feeling around.

"I told you I haven't got any money," the ugly woman said. "But if you keep doing that, I'll write you a check."

———————

The ugly woman screamed into the phone, "Send someone quick! Two naked bikers are climbing up toward my bedroom window!"

"This is the Fire Department, lady," the man said. "I'll have to transfer you to the Police Department."

"No, it's you I want," she yelled. "They need a longer ladder!"

A very homely woman made an appointment with a psychiatrist. She walked into his office and said, "Doctor, I'm so depressed and lonely. I don't have any friends, no man will touch me, and everybody laughs at me. Can you help me accept my ugliness?"

"Sure I can," the psychiatrist replied. "Just go over there and lie face down on the couch."

———————

How can you tell if a woman is fat?

When she has the mumps for two weeks and no one notices.

———————

How can you tell if a woman is flat?

When she has to have the word "front" tattooed on her chest.

———————

How can you tell if a woman is flat?

When she has to breast-feed through a straw.

How can you tell if a woman is really flat?

When you look down her dress, the biggest things you see are her corns.

———————————

How do you know if a woman's really flat?

Her biggest curve is a hemorrhoid.

———————————

What's the definition of ugly?

A girl who had to have tits grafted on her back to get laid.

———————————

How do you know your wife is really flat-chested?

She applies for a job as a topless waitress and they hire her as a busboy.

Chapter Six:

Gross Jokes about Loser Men

How do you know a guy's a loser?

When a hooker tells him she's got a headache.

———————

What's a real loser?

A guy whose hand falls asleep when he's masturbating.

Did you hear about the loser who finally turned to liquor as a substitute for women?

He got his dick caught in the mouth of a whiskey bottle.

———————

What's sex with a loser like?

Ever try stuffing a marshmallow into a parking-meter slot?

———————

Why do losers walk around with their flies open?

In case they have to count to eleven.

———————

The loser visited his parents the day after his wedding. His father took him aside and asked him, "How did it go last night, son?"

The loser winked and elbowed his Dad. "Gee, great. You know, the way she was acting, I think I could have fucked her."

How do you break a loser's finger?

Punch him in the nose.

_____

How do you get a loser to stop biting his nails?

Make him wear shoes.

_____

How can you tell if a guy's a loser?

When his idea of excitement is playing an AM radio in the afternoon.

_____

What's the definition of a black loser?

A guy who doesn't have carfare to get down to apply for welfare.

How can you tell if a guy in a singles bar is a loser?

His class ring is the pull top off a Budweiser can.

How do we know Adam was a loser?

Who else but a loser would stand next to a naked woman and just munch on an apple?

What's the definition of a loser?

A guy who rips off a girl's bra and starts biting her ear.

How can you tell a loser at an orgy?

He's the one who shows up with an artificial vagina as his date.

What's the difference between a pothole and a loser?

You'd swerve to avoid a pothole.

_____

How do you kill a loser?

Slam the toilet seat on his head when he's getting a drink of water.

_____

Why do losers wear hats?

So they know which end to wipe.

_____

Why don't losers clean their ears?

If they did, their heads would cave in.

What happens when a loser with an erection walks into a wall?

He smashes his nose.

———————————

What does a loser mean by a ménage à trois?

Using both hands to masturbate.

———————————

What's the cheapest way to grease your car?

Run over a loser.

———————————

What's another height of rejection for a loser?

He's masturbating and he goes limp.

How does a loser describe his sex life?

Fist or famine.

_____

What's a real loser?

A guy who has a wet dream and gets AIDS.

_____

What's a sure sign that you're bringing a loser home to bed?

When he assures you he'll be good for seconds.

_____

What did the loser do when his girlfriend asked him to do something kinky?

Shit in her purse.

How can you tell you're dating a real loser?

When he tries to buy his condoms from a bag lady.

What do you call a loser who always uses birth control?

A humanitarian.

Why do losers use their fingers to pick their noses?

Because their tongues aren't long enough.

What happened to the loser who learned to count to twenty-one?

He was arrested for indecent exposure.

What do you call the index finger of a loser's left hand?

A handkerchief.

———————

A loser went on vacation with his swinger friend. They were sunning on the beach when, to the loser's surprise, a gorgeous girl walked by and winked at him.

"Quick, what should I do?" he asked his friend.

"Wink back."

The loser winked back. The girl winked back and smiled.

"What should I do?" the loser asked again.

"Smile back."

The loser smiled back. Then the girl turned to face him, took off the top of her bikini, and lowered her panties.

The loser's eyes nearly came out of his head. "What should I do?" he demanded.

"Show her your nuts," the friend said.

So the loser stood up, put his thumbs in his ears, stuck out his tongue, and went "Blah . . . blah . . . blahhhhhh."

The loser was beating off as he stood in front of the full-length mirror. But try as he would, his member remained totally limp. "Damn," he swore as he finally walked away. "I guess I'm not my type."

———————————

How can you tell a loser at a ski resort?

He's the only one trying to get his pants on over his skis.

———————————

Why is a loser like Ronald Reagan?

When he finally gets in, he's got no idea what to do.

———————————

Did you hear about the loser who had a penis transplant?

His hand rejected it.

How can you tell a loser's got bad acne?

He falls asleep in the park and wakes up with a blind man reading his face.

_____

Did you hear about the loser who had an asshole transplant?

The asshole rejected him.

_____

Why are losers such lousy lovers?

Because they wait for the swelling to go down.

_____

The loser finally got married, but he had no idea what to do on his wedding night. His exasperated bride finally said, "Look, here's what you do. You take that thing that you play with and put it where I pee."

So the guy got up, found his bowling ball, and tossed it in the sink.

What do you call it when a loser makes a fist and kisses each knuckle?

Foreplay before masturbation.

What do you call a loser's right hand?

His sex organ.

What's the definition of dumb?

A guy who rolls up his sleeve when a girl says she wants to feel his muscle.

How can you tell if a guy's got a bad complexion?

He shaves with an ice-cream scoop.

How ugly was that guy?

If his dog wasn't blind, it would run away.

———————————

How can you tell if a guy is a real loser?

He has to put a pork chop around his neck to get a dog to play with him.

———————————

What does a loser play on his Walkman?

"Left, right, left, right, left, right . . ."

———————————

Did you hear about the new sex business for losers?

Self-service massage parlors.

Why should you be tolerant of losers who masturbate a lot?

They're only screwing themselves.

_____

How can you tell a guy is a real loser?

When blowing up an inflatable doll gives him a headache.

_____

What does a loser do with a pound of cocaine?

He snorts a gram and sells the rest to a narc.

_____

Why did the loser turn to drugs?

His shrink told him to find himself and girls kept telling him to get lost.

Why did God make semen white and urine yellow?

So losers could tell if they were coming or going.

———————————

How can you tell if a guy in a bar is a loser?

He sends a glass of water over to your table.

Chapter Seven:

A Gross Variety

A woman was cooking dinner when her little boy came into the kitchen and asked, "Mommy, why is Daddy so interested in the weather?"

She said, "Your father's not that interested in the weather. What makes you ask?"

"Well," the little boy said, "he's called Mrs. Simpson next door five times to ask if the coast was clear."

A guy walked into a bar, sat down, and ordered two double whiskeys. A friend said, "You look pissed. What's wrong?"

"It's that kid of mine. I think he's in love with his mother, like an Oedipus complex."

"How can you tell?"

"A few minutes ago I walked into his bedroom and found him masturbating."

"What's so unusual about that?"

"He was watching a Porky Pig video."

———————————

The little boy asked, "Mommy, where do babies come from?"

"You know that storks bring them," she replied.

"Yeah," the boy said. "But who fucks the storks?"

———————————

What do female snails say during sex?

"Faster, faster!"

A whale couple was swimming in the Pacific Ocean when they spotted a whaling ship in front of them. The male said to the other, "Hey, that's the ship that killed my parents! You've got to help me sink it."

The female said, "What do you have in mind?"

"We'll dive under the ship and blow hard through our blowholes. Then the ship will capsize."

The two whales dived, came up under the whaling vessel, and gave it a blast. Within moments, the entire crew was thrashing desperately in the waves. "Now," cried the first whale, "we're going to eat every one of those bastards!"

"Oh, no, we're not," said the female. "I don't mind blow jobs, but I'll be damned if I'll swallow seamen."

A mother was doing laundry one day when her eight-year-old daughter came down the basement stairs covered with blood and holding a knife in her hand. The mother screamed, "Jenny, you cut yourself!"

"Don't worry, Mom," the little girl said. "I was just helping my little brother."

"How could you help Jason with a knife?"

"You said Jason was a little devil. Well, I made him an angel."

What's the difference between eating sushi and eating pussy?

The rice.

What do Tupperware and male walruses have in common?

They both like a tight seal.

Why did the one-legged lady get raped?

She couldn't cross her legs to save her ass.

What's the worst business idea of the year?

A pet shop with "scratch and sniff" business cards.

What's black and white and red all over?

A panda on the rag.

———————————

If whiskey makes you frisky and gin makes you grin, what makes you pregnant?

Two highballs and a squirt.

Chapter Eight:

Gross Sex Jokes

Why should you be extra-nice to female executives?

You never know when they'll have an opening you could fill.

A guy walked into a bar a little before noon and to his surprise saw his buddy, a milkman, nursing a beer. He walked up and said, "Joe, you're never here before two or three. What's the problem?"

The milkman grumbled, "It's the God-damned recession."

"People aren't buying as much milk?"

"Nah," the milkman replied. "Twice as many husbands are home."

———————

What's the difference between a thirty-five-year-old woman and a thirty-five-year-old man?

A thirty-five-year-old woman is obsessed with having children; a thirty-five-year-old man is obsessed with fucking children.

———————

What's the best gift for a woman who has everything?

A man to show her how to work it.

Why are men like pantyhose?

They both cling to women, but one rough spot, and watch them run.

———————————

Why are women like babies?

When they start to cry, they're usually full of shit.

———————————

How do you get a man to spend more time on foreplay?

A longer half time.

What's the only way to make men concerned about the environment?

Tell them there's a global beer shortage.

Why is the average man like Colonel Sanders?

All he cares about is legs, breasts, and thighs.

What's a perfect blind date?

A woman who comes to the door naked and holding a six-pack.

Two women were having coffee when one complained, "I've just about had it with Fred."

"What's wrong?"

"He's the worst lover in the world. I spend half an hour fussing and primping before bed. Then he walks in, flips off his underwear, climbs on top, pumps away for thirty seconds, then rolls off and starts snoring."

"I had the same problem with Bill," the other woman said. "Then I found this marvelous book. Once I got him to read it, our sex life turned fabulous."

The first woman's eyes brightened. "Let me borrow it."

A week later, the two women met again. The woman who lent the book started to speak but her friend said, "Don't ask. I'm filing for divorce."

"What happened? Wouldn't he look at the book?"

"When I said it would improve his sex life, he looked. Then he handed it back to me and said, 'It won't work.' I asked him why. He said, 'Because there's no telephone numbers in it.'"

The seventeen-year-old gas-station attendant looked like an Adonis, but he came from a strict, religious family. That's why he blushed furiously when the thirty-five-year-old blond customer came on to him. She ran her fingers down the front of his shirt and said, "Now, wouldn't you like to fool around?"

He stammered, "N-n-n-no, ma'am. I'm not allowed to touch women."

She thought for a moment, then said, "Well, let's pretend I'm a car." She unzipped his pants and pulled out his dick, which rapidly grew rigid. She then said, "And this is your dipstick. Now, I insist you check my fluids." She pulled up her skirt and guided him inside her. Unable to help himself, the young lad pumped furiously for a moment before he came.

Ashamed, he tried to pull away. But she grabbed his still-erect member and said, "You've got to do it again."

"Why?" he protested.

"Because," she explained, pointing to his dick, "according to this, I'm still half a quart low."

How can you tell if the guy you're marrying has a big ego?

The wedding cake has only a statue of him.

———————

Three women were sitting around talking about their sex lives. The first said, "I think my husband's like a championship golfer. He's spent the last ten years perfecting his stroke."

The second woman said, "My husband's like the winner of the Indianapolis 500. Everytime we get into bed he gives me several hundred exciting laps."

The third woman was silent until she was asked, "Tell us about your husband, Jill." She thought for a moment, then said, "My husband's like an Olympic gold-medal-winning quarter-miler."

"How so?"

"He's got his time down to under forty seconds."

Why do most husbands like to keep the lights on during sex?

They're less likely to blurt out the wrong name.

What's the main thing you learn from fucking your wife?

Sometimes, nothing is better than something.

A guy walked into a bar and a friend said, "Hey, Fred. I haven't seen you in a long time. You look terrific."

"Thanks," Fred said, "I owe it all to my doctor."

"What did he do?"

"Well, I went in for a checkup a month or so ago, and he told me that I'd live a lot longer if my life was totally fat-free."

"So you changed your diet?"

"Diet, hell," Fred said. "I went home and threw out my wife."

Two women were chatting when one said, "My husband finally found a way to satisfy me."

"Really?" her friend said.

"Yeah. He's sleeping in the guest bedroom."

Why is telephone sex a billion-dollar business?

Men are all talk.

Why don't men make eye contact?

Tits don't have eyes.

Did you hear about the new chain of combination saunas and massage parlors?

It's called the "Steam and Cream."

How do you know if your date suffers from premature ejaculation?

When he comes walking through the door.

Why do women love working in the impotency clinic?

It's a soft job.

The husband came home from work early one night, handed his wife a bouquet, and said, "Say, wanna have a quickie?"

She looked at him with a puzzled expression and asked, "As opposed to what?"

One guy ran into a friend at the pool hall and said, "Ralph, are you still going to those wife-swapping parties?"

"Nah," Ralph said. "It didn't work out?"

"You mean, you missed your wife?"

"No," Ralph replied, "It was way too depressing when I got her back."

———————————

The phone rang at 3:00 A.M. When he picked up the phone, a voice said, "Dad, you have to come down to the police station and get me. I got arrested for doing 69 in your Cadillac."

"I told you not to take that vehicle on the highway," the father roared.

"I didn't take it on the highway," his son protested. "Hell, I never left the parking lot."

———————————

Why did they cancel National Orgasm Week?

Most people only pretended to celebrate.

What's embarrassing?

A wife's Ben-Wa balls set off the airport metal detector.

What's more embarrassing?

Your penile implant sets off the airport metal detector.

How do you know your sex life is lousy?

For Christmas, you wife gives you an erection set.

Did you hear about the new radio station WPMS?

Every month they play two weeks of love songs, one week of blues and one week of ragtime.

The women were sitting around playing bridge when the hostess's husband came down and said, "Honey, I'm off to the golf course. How about a good-bye kiss?"

"All right," she said, "Come over here." He complied. Then, to the astonishment of the other women, she unzipped his fly, pulled out his penis, kissed it on the head, and tucked it back in his pants.

For a moment after he left, the ladies sat in shocked silence. Finally, one asked, "Why did you do that?"

The hostess replied calmly, "Have you ever smelled his breath?"

The couple was sitting at the bar when a voluptuous blonde passed. Noting that the guy couldn't keep his eyes off of her, the girl said, "That's only Marla Epstein. She gets her good looks from her father."

The guy said, "Don't you mean, from her mother?"

"No, her father—he's a plastic surgeon."

A guy was downing doubles at the bar when a friend asked, "What's wrong, Hal?"

Hal grimaced, "I just signed my divorce settlement."

"What kind of split did you get?"

"Fifty-fifty," he replied.

The friend said, "That sounds fair."

Hal grunted. "My ex-wife got half and my lawyer got half."

Did you hear about the revolutionary new artificial vagina?

It's called, "I Can't Believe It's Not Pussy."

The male bodybuilder eyed a gorgeous female lifting weights in the gym. He ambled over and said, "Hey, babe. What do you say to a little private training session?"

She replied, "What do you have in mind?"

He stared at her crotch and said, "I feel like working on the snatch."

She retorted, "I think you should head for the shower."

"Why?"

She pointed at his groin and said, "You'll have to settle for the clean and jerk."

———————————

The couple left the singles bar and went to her apartment, where he was soon thrusting and grunting away. After a few minutes, the guy asked, "So, how am I?"

The women said, "You make love like you were three guys."

"I told you I was great," he bragged.

She added, "And those three guys are Curly, Larry, and Moe."

What's the smallest cemetery in the world?

A woman's cunt—it only takes one stiff at a time.

———————————

A mother walked into her daughter's house to find the recently married girl thumbing furiously through the Yellow Pages.

"What are you doing?" the mother asked.

"Fred's birthday is Saturday," the girl replied. "He told me to buy him whatever he needed the most."

"So what's the problem?" the mother asked.

"I've looked through this book three times," said the bride. "Where in the hell can I buy him six more inches?"

———————————

Why are electric trains like a woman's tits?

They're intended for children, but it's the fathers who play with them.

A man got friendly with a woman at the hotel bar and took her to his room. They started to fool around, and soon he discovered that she had a huge cunt. Eventually, she took all her clothes off, lay down on her back, and opened her legs wide.

The man looked at her and said, "Take it easy, babe. I usually fuck from the outside in, not the other way around."

The wife sat up in bed and asked her husband, "Why don't you ever go down on me?"

"I don't know," the husband replied. "I just don't want to."

"Is it because you don't think my cunt is clean?" the wife asked.

"What?" the husband replied.

"I said, don't you think my cunt is clean?"

"What?"

"Herb, are you deaf?"

"Sorry," the husband shouted. "I can't hear you. The flies are buzzing too loudly."

Why does a piece of ass cost $50 when a human body is only worth about $7.28?

Because a hole is worth more than the sum of its parts.

———————————

Why do men have a knob on the end of their penises?

To keep their hand from falling off.

———————————

How can you tell if a girl's got a huge cunt?

When you can use her IUD as a hula hoop.

———————————

How do men put on their underwear?

Yellow stains in front, brown in the rear.

Why are women amazing?

They give milk without eating hay, they bleed without being cut, and they bury bones without digging a hole.

A woman hailed a cab one night. When the taxi pulled up in front of her apartment building, she realized she'd forgotten her purse. She said to the driver, "I don't have any money." She lifted up her skirt spread her legs, pulled down her panties, then added, "Will you take it out in trade?"

The cabbie turned around to look, then grimaced. "Lady, don't you have anything smaller?"

Why did Moses get so upset when God was talking to him on Mount Sinai?

He said, "You mean we're the chosen people, and we have to cut off the tips of our what?"

Why did God give women nipples?

To make suckers out of men.

Two professors were talking one evening. One said, "I just translated an old German myth that might interest you. It said that in the beginning of time, men and women were built exactly alike, and they complained of having nothing to do. So the gods sent an elf to hide under a bridge with a golden hatchet, and he was instructed to gash every other person that walked overhead. Of course, some people were tall, and the elf had to reach high, so they only got small gashes. Some people were the right height, and they got perfect gashes, while short people really got split."

The other professor exclaimed, "That explains it. My wife must have scooted across the bridge on her ass."

Did you hear about the guy whose wife nagged so much even her cunt talked back?

She called it her answering cervix.

What did the single guy mean when he said he liked women who were musical types?

They were fit as a fiddle and tight as a drum.

Why don't women have their hair on their chests?

Did you ever see grass growing on a playground?

The teenager went to a whorehouse for the first time, and ended up with one of the older hookers. They went upstairs. She undressed, then parted her legs. When he saw her vagina, he burst out laughing.

"Hey," she complained, "what are you laughing at? You came out of one of these."

"I know," the kid said, "But that's the first one I've seen that I could crawl back into."

A guy who'd had more than a few drinks staggered onto the airplane. When the stewardess came by, he unzipped his pants and leered at her.

She took a quick glance, then said, "Mac, I need to see your ticket, not your stub."

———————

Why do some women prefer jellybeans to men?

Jellybeans come in eight delicious colors.

———————

What's the difference between dark and hard?

It stays dark all night long.

What did the left tit say to the right tit?

"We'd better stop sagging so low or they'll think we're nuts."

Why is a penis like Rubik's Cube?

The longer you play with it, the harder it gets.

An architect, an engineer, and a city planner were having some drinks and talking about women. The conversation came around to the subject of who designed a woman's body.

The architect said, "It must have been someone in my profession. Look at the beauty of the lines."

The engineer disagreed. "It had to have been someone with engineering training. The body's so well-proportioned and so functional."

"You're both wrong," the third man said. "It had to have been a city planner who designed women. Who else would have put the playground so close to the waste disposal?"

Did you hear that legs are a girl's best friends?

Yes, but even the best of friends must part.

_____

What is sixteen inches long, white and hard?

Nothing.

_____

Why is a suntanned girl like a roast chicken?

The white meat is the best.

A steelworker reported for work one morning at a housing project in Harlem when his supervisor said to him, "Hey, Tony, you look like shit. You feel okay?"

"Fine," Tony replied. He started working, when his partner said, "Man, you look awful. You ought to see a doctor."

Tony again protested that he felt fine. But by lunchtime so many people had told him how terrible he looked that he started to be a little worried. Then the boss came by and said, "Tony, I can't take a chance on you infecting the whole crew. There's a doctor's office across the street. I insist you get yourself checked."

Tony protested, but a few minutes later he walked across the street and into the very dingy office of "Doctor Voodoo." The old black man who came out looked very crazy, but Tony was under strict orders to get himself checked. He told the old man what had happened.

"You is in luck," the old man said. "I just gots a new book of symptoms." He turned the pages slowly, mumbling to himself, "Looks bad, feels bad. Looks good, feels good. Looks good, feels bad—ah, here it be. Looks bad, feels good."

Tony said impatiently, "Tell me, Doc. What do I have?"

"It says here," the doc said, "that if you look bad and feels good, you's a vagina."

Why is a woman like a toilet seat?

Without a hole in the middle, she wouldn't be good for shit.

———————

How can you tell if a girl has a huge cunt?

Her gynecologist is a member of the United Mine Workers.

———————

How do you know girls aren't made of sugar and spice?

They taste like anchovies.

Why shouldn't a girl be too upset when she loses her cherry?

She's still got the box it came in.

How do you know a guy's got a small dick?

When he can fuck Cheerios and they don't break.

The big attraction at the State Fair was a cow reportedly worth one million dollars. "Why is that cow worth so much money?" a curious farmer asked another man standing in line to see the animal.

"Because," the man replied, "if you stand real close, you can see that the cow has a pussy just like a woman's."

The farmer started to roar with laughter. The man stared at him, then finally asked, "What's so funny?"

The farmer shook his head. "Just to think. I got a wife with a pussy like a cow's, and she isn't worth a darned cent."

A teenage boy was sitting on the porch of the country store with an old man. After a while, the boy said to his elder, "I want to learn all about women. What do you call that little button in a woman's slit?"

"That's a clitoris," the old man replied.

"And what's the brown part around the nipples?" The old man replied, "That's the aureola."

"Wow," the boy exclaimed, "you know everything. How about the name of that smooth patch of skin between a woman's cunt and her asshole?"

The old man said, "Around here, we call that the chin rest."

———————

A guy was boasting at a bar about his wonderful sense of smell. Soon wagers were placed, and the man blindfolded. One of the other patrons placed a flower under his nose. The man sniffed and said, "That's a lily."

Another man came up with a twig. It took the sniffer a couple of minutes, but he correctly said, "That's a branch from a maple tree." Several more guesses emptied the pockets of the other patrons. Finally, the bartender called the waitress over, ran his finger inside her panties, then stuck it under the sniffer's nose. "What's that?" he asked.

"Fish," the man replied.

Why do women rub their eyes when they wake up in the morning?

Because they don't have balls to scratch.

Why do women have legs?

So they don't leave snail trails when they walk.

The couple were driving along in the mountains when the woman asked her husband to stop the car so she could take a shit. He pulled over a little while later and told her to shit off a footbridge over a river.

She complied. A few minutes later, she called out, "Fred, come here. I'm afraid I just shit into a canoe."

He came running over, then looked down into the water. "You idiot," he said, "That's not a canoe. That's the reflection of your cunt."

How can you tell if a woman's tits really sag?

When she feels a lump in her breast and discovers it's her shoe.

What's the difference between parsley and pussy?

Nobody eats parsley.

Why do women have cunts?

So men will talk to them.

A guy and a girl are making out in the living room, and both are getting charged up. "Put your finger inside me," the girl pants. He does it.

"Put another finger inside me," she moans.

He does it.

"Put your hand inside me," she demands. Then, "Put your other hand inside me."

He does what she asks.

"Now clap," she orders.

"I can't," he protests.

"Tight, huh?" she smiles.

———————

Why is pubic hair curly?

You'd poke your eye out if it were straight.

———————

What's the dumbest part of a man?

His prick—its got no brains, its best friends are two nuts, and it lives next door to an asshole.

What's the fuction of a woman?

A life-support system for a pussy.

_____

How do you know God meant for man to eat pussy?

He made it look like a taco.

_____

What is the only thing the government can't tax?

A penis—90% of the time it's unemployed, 10% of the time it's in the hole, and it's got two dependents and they're both nuts.

_____

What do a cobra and a one-inch cock have in common?

No one wants to fuck with either one of them.

Why shouldn't you suck a twelve-inch cock?

You get foot-in-mouth disease.

———————————

Why is life like a penis?

Because when it's soft, it's hard to beat, but when it's hard, you get screwed.

———————————

How many animals can you find in a pair of pantyhose?

Two calves, ten little piggies, one ass, one pussy, a thousand hares, maybe some crabs, and a dead fish no one can find.

———————————

Why is a clitoris like Antarctica?

Most men know it's there, but few really care.

One day a man was sunbathing on a nude beach when he noticed a little girl staring at him. So he put a newspaper over his private parts. The girl came up and asked him what was under the newspaper. He said, "That's my bird, and I keep it there so it won't fly away."

Then the guy fell asleep. When he woke up, however, he found himself in a hospital room. The little girl was still with him, so he asked her, "What happened?"

The little girl said, "While you were sleeping, I started to play with your bird. But it spit at me, so I broke its neck, crushed its eggs, and set fire to its nest."

The guy walked into the furrier's store and announced, "I want to buy a fur for my wife."

"Mink?" the salesman asked.

"She's got one."

"Fox?"

"She's got one."

"Skunk?"

"Skunk?" the customer asked.

"Why not? It's just a pussy that smells bad."

The customer said, "She's got one of those, too."

Did you hear about the new male hygiene deodorant called Umpire?

It gets rid of foul balls.

Why do men sleep better on their sides?

They have a kickstand.

What's the new male horror movie?

Chain Saw Vasectomy.

The washing machine broke down one day, and the woman didn't have any clean underwear. So she went shopping without panties on. Her second stop was a shoe store, and the salesman serving her really enjoyed the view. He kept his excitement to himself for a while, but finally he couldn't resist exclaiming, "You have a beautiful pussy, and I'd love to eat ice cream out of it."

Shocked, the woman ran out of the store and called her husband, urging him to go down to the store and beat up the salesman. The husband replied, "No way I'm going down there, for three reasons. First of all, you shouldn't have been out without panties. Secondly, you already own fifty pairs of shoes. And thirdly, anybody who can eat that much ice cream is too big to fuck with."

———————

If God made the top half of a woman, who designed the bottom?

A black. Who else would give it big lips, kinky hair, and a smell like a catfish?

Did you hear about the guy who got a vasectomy at Sears?

Every time he gets an erection, his garage door opens.

Why is a cock like a snake?

It's long and thin,
It's covered with skin,
And God only knows what holes it's been in.

Chapter Nine

Simply Disgusting

How did the hillbilly girl know when her mother had her period?

Her brother's dick tasted funny.

———————————

What's the difference between male bonding and female bonding?

Female bonding doesn't require throwing up in the back seat.

How do you know you have bad breath?

The dentist takes laughing gas.

———————————

The military plane crashed into the Pacific and the only two survivors, a man and a woman, made it to an uninhabited island. They were almost instantly attracted to each other, and their love made their situation bearable as they built a large hut, cultivated food, and tamed some wild goats and pigs as livestock.

But about a year later, shortly after the birth of their child, the man began to get homesick. He went on and on about how he'd like to be back in the city, sitting at a ball game, drinking beer and eating a hot dog. Finally, his obsession got so strong that the woman couldn't stand it anymore. One day, he came back from collecting water to find that she had made a chair for him out of bamboo. "Just like a ball-park seat," she said. "Sit."

Surprised, he sat down. She disappeared for a moment, then she came back in wearing a hat and shouting, "Get your beer, ice cold beer." She handed him a cup. He took a sip and said, "This tastes great. What is it?"

She said, "I've been experimenting for months until I got the perfect recipe using wild rice and fruit. I cooled it in the lagoon."

"That's great," he said. "But . . ."

"I know," she said. She left the hut, then returned, shouting, "Hot dogs, get your hot dogs." She handed him a bun.

He took a bite, then said, "How did you get this?"

She hesitated a second, then said, "Well, I hope you're not turned off, but that hot dog is really a pig's penis."

To her delight, he said, "So who cares what part of a pig I eat. It tastes like the real thing. And how did you get this yellow mustard."

"Oh, that," she said, "It's baby shit."

———————

The State Supreme Court upheld the new death penalty act and advertised for a new executioner. With unemployment at a record high, more than 1,000 people applied. Because electrocution would be used, the state finally selected Fred Jones, an electrical engineer who had seven kids to support.

Jones spent two weeks refurbishing the sixty-year-old electric chair. But, to his horror, it blew fuses every time he tested it. With the first execution the next morning, he thought he'd blown it. Later that night, he staggered home drunk. Before he passed out, he told his family, "I'm going to lose my job and we'll lose this house."

He woke up with a terrific hangover, but his wife insisted he report to work. His heart was in his throat as the condemned man was strapped in. But when he pulled the lever, the chair functioned perfectly.

Elated, he called home. When his oldest son answered, he said, "The chair worked! My job is saved!"

"I know," the teenager said. "After you passed out last night, I went down to the prison to work on it."

"But how did you know it would work?"

"That was the tough part," the boy said. "I fried Sally, Janey, and the twins before I was sure."

The hire-the-handicapped program had gotten off to a slow start, and the director was particularly upset that not one quadripleigic had been hired. He decided to go door-to-door to drum up some jobs. He met with no luck until he came to the largest farm in the county. The farmer came to the door, listened to the director's plea, then said, "Well, maybe I can help. What can these quadripleigics do?"

"Well," the director said, "they have no feeling or movement from the neck down. But they can talk— they can operate special telephones—and they can type using a computer tied to their eye movement. We supply the special equipment free of charge."

"I won't be needing the equipment," the farmer said. "But if they can talk, I'll hire ten of them."

The next morning, a van took the ten paralyzed workers to the farm. But the director began to wonder how in heaven's name a farmer could use them. He drove out to the farm to see, but the farmer said,

"They're not here. They're out working in the fields."

"You mean they're operating tractors?"

"Hell, no," the farmer said. "We nailed them all to crosses. Best scarecrows I ever had."

———————

Two streetwalkers were picked up by two guys in a beat-up Chevy. They parked at the docks, and began administering their $10 blow jobs. After a couple of minutes, one looked up and said to her john, "Hey, I'll bet you're from Maryland."

The guy was amazed. "How in the hell can you tell?"

The hooker said, "Your crotch. It's crawling with soft-shelled crabs."

———————

The surgical team had frantically opened the skull of the Polish accident victim, hoping to relieve pressure from a concussion. The drill had no sooner penetrated the layer of bone than a horrible odor permeated the operating room. The head surgeon took a look, then said, "Someone had better get a video camera in here—we've made a scientific discovery."

"What's that?" another doctor said.
"Polacks really do have shit for brains."

———————

How do you get a Polish girl pregnant?

Come on her shoes and let the flies do the rest.

———————

The loser couldn't get anywhere with girls because of his horrible breath. He went to his doctor for an exam. The doctor told him, "I'm afraid you need a psychiatrist instead."

"Why a psychiatrist?"

"You have to break one of your two bad habits—you either have to stop scratching your ass or biting your fingernails."

———————

How can you tell if a guy's got weak kidneys?

Rusty zipper and yellow socks.

A guy was sitting next to a friend and said, "I gotta leave my wife."

"What's the problem?"

"Well, she's gotten fat and lazy."

"So, whose wife hasn't?" the friend asked.

"But my wife has a bowel movement every morning at seven."

"What does that have to do with you?"

"She's so lazy she doesn't get out of bed until nine."

A pretty young teenage girl, a single girl in her midtwenties, and a married woman walked into a lingerie shop to buy a new set of panties. The saleswoman asked the teenage girl how many she needed.

"Seven," the young thing replied, "One for each day of the week."

The saleswoman got her order, then asked the same question of the single girl.

"I need one each day for Monday through Friday," the single girl replied. "On weekends, my lover and I spend so much time in bed I don't need panties."

The saleswoman gave her five pairs, then said to the married woman, "How many pairs do you need?"

"Twelve," the married woman replied. "January, February, March . . ."

How do you recondition an old wife?

Slam a ten-pound ham up her cunt and pull out the bone.

———————————

Two men were brought to court for fighting. One guy defended himself by saying, "That bastard made me hit him. He said my wife was the ugliest, dirtiest, smelliest, old whore in town."

The judge replied, "That's terrible. Why don't you bring your wife down to testify against him, too?"

The guy suddenly looked uncomfortable. "Uh, your honor . . . I'd like to know one thing. Will it hurt my case if he's telling the truth?"

Wilma was frustrated over her lousy sex life, so she talked to her next-door neighbor. The neighbor asked Judy what she wore to bed.

"I have this white nightgown with a high lacy front and a low-cut back. George used to think it was sexy, but now he doesn't even look at me."

"Turn it around so it's cut low in front," the neighbor advised. "It's sure to turn George on."

That night, George climbed into bed and turned on the news, as usual. Wilma went into the bathroom, put on her nightgown backwards, moved seductively out the door and across the room, turned off the TV, got into bed, and nibbled on George's ear.

George just grunted and rolled over.

Wilma slapped him on the arm. "George, I want to make love," she said. "Don't you notice anything different about my nightgown?"

"Yeah," he said. "The shit stains are on the front."

———————————

Why do women fart after they pee?

They can't shake it, so they have to blow-dry it.

A young cannibal girl was helping with the feast for the first time. She watched as a missionary was lowered into a stew pot. Her mother turned to her and said, "I'm going to let you help with dinner tonight. It's much easier when we're serving a man."

"How's that?" the girl asked.

The mother replied, "All you have to do is watch until his balls explode—then you add the potatoes and vegetables."

———————

What's flat, squishy, and soaks the ground with blood and excrement?

A Polish skydiver.

———————

What hits the water at speeds of sixty miles per hour?

A Polish bungee jumper.